SMOKING

Sally Morgan

RAINTREE
STECK-VAUGHN
PUBLISHERS

A Harcourt Company

Austin   New York
www.raintreesteckvaughn.com

**Library of Congress Cataloging-in-Publication
Data is available upon request.**

ISBN 0-7398-4774-0

Printed in Italy. Bound in the United States.

1 2 3 4 5 6 7 8 9 0 LB 05 04 03 02 01

Acknowledgments
The author and publishers thank the following for their permission to reproduce photographs and
illustrations: John Birdsall Photography: page 21 (library photo); Camera Press: pages 43, 48; Corbis
Images: pages 4b, 53 (Duncan Smith); Ecoscene: pages 6 (Christine Osborne), 22 (Christine
Osborne), 25 (Chinch Gryniewicz); Angela Hampton Family Life Pictures: pages 19, 20, 22, 47, 52,
55; Peter Newark's American Pictures: page 8; Photofusion: page 54 (Peter Olive); Pictorial Press:
pages 16, 45; Popperfoto: pages 14, 28, 49, 59; Chris Schwarz: page 9; Science Photo Library: pages
4t (Bill Barksdale/Agstock), 5 (Oscar Burriel), 35 (Department of Clinical Radiology, Salisbury
District Hospital), 39 (Larry Mulvehill), 40 (James Stevenson), 46 (Mark Clarke); Steve Skjold: page
58; Tony Stone Images: pages 7 (Zigy Kaluzny); Topham Picturepoint: pages 12, 17, 18, 44, 57;
Wayland Picture Library: pages 10, 13, 23, 26, 30, 32 (Michael Courtney), 37 (Michael Courtney), 38
(Michael Courtney), 50; White-Thomson: page 31t, 31b.

Contents

Introduction
The Origins

Tobacco has been smoked, sniffed, and chewed for hundreds of years. The tobacco plant originated in North America, where Native Americans used it. Spanish explorers brought tobacco to Europe at the end of the 15th century, and its use spread rapidly in some social circles, partly because it was thought to have medicinal value. It was smoked first in pipes and later in cigarettes, which appeared during the mid-19th century and were far more convenient to smoke. This led to an increase in the popularity of smoking, which became a familiar and popular social activity around the world. Today, about one-third of all people aged 15 or over smoke. That's a staggering total of 1.1 billion and the number is still increasing.

Tobacco plants
These tobacco plants flourish in North Carolina.

"Healing powers"
The Elizabethans were so impressed by the miraculous healing powers of the "divine tobacco" leaf that they called it herb panacea—the plant to cure all diseases. Native Americans, who had chewed, snorted, and smoked tobacco for hundreds of years, believed that tobacco had many medicinal and magical properties. They believed that its powers were greater if it was smoked.

Medicinal uses
Smoking tobacco was advertised to 19th-century New Yorkers as a cure for many respiratory illnesses.

A Consumer Product That Can Kill

Smoking is rarely out of the news. Over the last 50 years, thousands of scientific articles have been written showing that smoking causes lung and heart disease, premature death, and disability. More recently, there have been campaigns to ban smoking from public places to protect non-smokers from the dangers of inhaling other people's smoke. There are strict regulations relating to the advertising of tobacco products. There are also a number of high-profile court cases in North America and Europe, where people suffering from smoking-related diseases are suing the tobacco companies for damages. And every year there are "stop smoking" campaigns to help people kick the habit. It's strange to think that tobacco is the only legally available consumer product that kills people when it is used entirely as intended.

About This Book

Most of you reading this book will be familiar with and be able to relate to the issues covered because you know someone who smokes, are a smoker yourself, or are an ex-smoker. Chapter 1 looks at why people start to smoke and how advertising, the media, and role models can influence young people. Chapter 2 examines the cigarette itself, the chemicals found in tobacco and their effect on the body, especially the addictive nature of nicotine. In Chapter 3 there is a detailed examination of the effects of smoking on health, and Chapter 4 shows how inhaling someone else's smoke (passive smoking) can harm the health of non-smokers and unborn babies. Chapter 5 considers ways in which a smoker can kick the smoking habit. Sources of information and support are listed on pages 60-61 and the Glossary on page 62 explains less familiar terms.

Heart disease
A modern-day image warns that smoking increases the risk of heart disease.

1 Why Smoke?
Background, Pressures, and Choices

Increasing Numbers of Smokers

There are an estimated 1.1 billion smokers in the world, and of these more than 800 million live in developing countries. If the number of people who smoke continues to increase at the current rate, it is predicted that by 2025 there will be a total of 1.64 billion smokers.

The pattern in the increase in the number of smokers around the world is not uniform, however, and there is a distinct difference between developed and developing countries. Between 1981 and 1991, the number of cigarettes smoked fell in developed countries but rose in the developing world. It is still increasing there at a rate of about 3.4 percent a year.

Malaysia
A group of Malaysian college students relax with cigarettes.

In Great Britain, the number of smokers peaked in 1972, when almost half of the population smoked. Since then there has been a decline in the number of smokers, especially among older generations. Now smokers make up less than one-third of the population. However, young people are still taking up smoking and replacing older people who are stopping. In contrast, smoking is increasing rapidly in China. Between 1970 and 1992 there, the consumption of cigarettes per adult rose by 260 percent. There are now about 300 million Chinese smokers, of whom 90 percent are men.

Teenagers
Some young people smoke as a form of rebellion against the rules at home or at school.

Gender and Social Class

There are differences in the numbers of male and female smokers. More than one-quarter of smokers in developed countries are women, compared with just one in 14 in developing countries.

There are differences between social classes in all parts of the world. In general, men and women classed as unskilled manual labor are more likely to smoke than people classed as professional. Approximately 12 percent of men and 11

World cigarette consumption

As you would expect, trillions of cigarettes are smoked each year. In 1998, world production of cigarettes was a massive 5.61 trillion—the equivalent of 948 cigarettes per person or 2.6 cigarettes per day for every man, woman, and child.

The largest manufacturer in the world is the state-owned China National Tobacco Corporation, which accounted for one-third of global cigarette production (1.7 trillion cigarettes) in 1997, followed by Philip Morris, in the United States, and British American Tobacco.

percent of women in the professional group smoke, compared with 41 percent of men and 36 percent of women in the unskilled manual group.

Why Do People Smoke?

Given that so many people smoke, there must be some strong reasons for starting. Some of these are:

- to calm their nerves
- to help them during stressful times
- to help them to lose weight
- to give them something to do with their hands
- to make them look cool
- because their friends or family smoke.

There was a surge in the number of smokers during both World Wars. People led incredibly stressful lives in the war years and, not surprisingly, many turned to tobacco. Furthermore, during World War II, cigarettes were included in the ration packs (items such as food and cigarettes given to soldiers during wartime) of the armed forces. In Europe,

GIs
A war reporter hands cigarettes to U.S. soldiers in Okinawa, Japan in 1945.

the influence of the GIs (American soldiers), most of whom smoked, led to many people taking up the habit. The GIs gave packs of cigarettes along with pairs of silk stockings to their girlfriends. The result was a generation of smokers who, at that time, were unaware of the dangers of smoking to their health.

Teenage Smoking

Surprisingly, few adults take up smoking. Most smokers start the habit in their adolescent years. In Great Britain and the United States, almost one-quarter of 15-year-olds, both boys and girls, are regular smokers. Each day, 3,000 young people (teenagers and younger) in the United States and 450 in Great Britain smoke their first cigarette. During the 1980s, the number of young people who smoked leveled off and even started to fall, but in the early 1990s there was a sudden upturn that continued until the end of the decade. Then in Great Britain the numbers fell again, but in the United States they are still rising.

So what encourages a young person to smoke a cigarette for the first time? The three most important factors are

Showing the way
A child of parents who smoke is very likely to become a smoker, too.

parents, siblings, and friends. You are three times as likely to smoke if both your parents smoke. Parental opinion is a major factor. If you believe that your parents disapprove of smoking, you are less likely to become a smoker. An older brother or sister who smokes also has a strong influence. A younger sibling is more likely to experiment with cigarettes and may even obtain cigarettes from the brother or sister. Friends are the greatest influence in teenage smoking. Teenagers may smoke because they want to belong to a particular group. Others may lack the skills to refuse a cigarette offered by a friend or someone they would like to be their friend.

"There's a small group of smokers at school. They stand in a huddle and pass cigarettes around." (Claire, 13)

Which Children Are Most Likely to Become Smokers?

A survey of more than 2,000 children aged 12–13 was undertaken in 1988 to predict the onset of smoking. The main factors influencing a young person's decision to smoke are given in order of importance.

Boys

1. having a best friend who smokes
2. knowing at least one cigarette brand
3. having a favorite cigarette advertisement
4. not knowing or accepting any health risks
5. having at least one parent who smokes

Girls

1. having at least one parent who smokes
2. having positive views about what smoking will do for them; for example, it gives confidence, calms nerves, controls weight
3. knowing at least one cigarette brand
4. having a best friend who smokes
5. not knowing or accepting any health risks

How 9–18–year-olds view smoking

	PERCENTAGES OF	
POSITIVE VIEWS	REGULAR SMOKERS	NEVER SMOKED
Smoking calms your nerves	72	29
Smoking keeps your weight down	39	17
Smoking gives you confidence	36	10
Smoking is fun	29	1
Smoking makes you feel grown-up	24	24
Smoking makes you look tough	12	20
NEGATIVE VIEWS		
Smoking is a waste of money	75	95
Smoking makes you smelly	63	77
Young people smoke to "show off"	36	76

Stages in Smoking

Young smokers go through a series of stages and each one is influenced by different factors.

1. Precontemplation

The young person is not thinking about smoking, but receives messages about it. At this stage, the person is influenced by parents, siblings, and friends who may smoke, as well as by advertising, smoking in films and on television, and smoking by role models.

"There are always cigarettes lying around our house. One day I was on my own and I tried one." (Jamie, 14)

2. Contemplation

The influence of friends, family, and media builds up to a point where curiosity takes over and the young person considers trying a cigarette.

3. Initiation

Most young people will try smoking, but the majority do not become regular smokers. At this stage, friends are usually the strongest influence.

4. Experimentation

There may be repeated attempts to smoke. Young people can become addicted to nicotine after smoking a very small number of cigarettes, which is why many experimenters become regular smokers. At this stage, peer pressure is still the strongest influence.

5. Regular Smoking

This may involve a new set of influences. As well as addiction and habituation, personal factors such as beliefs about the benefits of smoking and self-perception have an effect. Factors such as cost, availability, and school policy all play their role.

6. Maintenance

The continuation of regular smoking involves all these influences, but addiction is a major force.

7. Quitting

This occurs when the relative importance of influences changes. A decision to stop can be triggered by, for example, a new non-smoking friend, a steep increase in the price of cigarettes, a decrease in spending money, or even working in an office where smoking is not permitted.

Belonging

Is it necessary to do the same as a group of friends, to feel that you are part of the group?

Advertising Techniques

Advertising can play an important role when a young person makes the all-important decision to smoke his or her first cigarette. Research shows that young people usually smoke the brands that are promoted most heavily. A survey in California in 1996 interviewed just under 1,800 people between the ages of 12 and 17. None of them had ever smoked. When interviewed again three years later, the researchers discovered that 30 percent had tried a cigarette, 16 percent were willing to smoke, and 3 percent were smokers. Those who had been able to name a cigarette brand in 1996 were twice as likely to have started, or be willing to start, smoking than those who had not been able to. The three most advertised brands in the United States have a 35 percent market share. But 86 percent of underage smokers choose these brands, indicating that young people are heavily influenced by advertising. The importance of advertising to young consumers was evident during 1989

Adventure

This image appeared on an advertisement for cigarettes which were claimed to have the "taste of adventure."

and 1993, when spending on promoting the Joe Camel brand in the United States leapt from $27 million to $43 million. This highly successful campaign resulted in a 50 percent increase in Camel's share of the youth market. In contrast, it had little impact on the adult market.

Advertising also creates the impression that smoking is a normal, socially acceptable habit. In 1965, cigarette advertising was banned from television in Great Britain. In 1991, this was extended across the European Union (EU). As a result, cigarette manufacturers started to sponsor sports, such as motor racing, pool, and rugby, as an alternative way of advertising their brands on television. Young people watching these events on television, or at a venue like a concert, cannot miss the advertising posters and banners, and they subconsciously link smoking with the healthy lifestyle associated with sports. One study in Great Britain found that boys whose favorite sport was automobile racing were twice as likely to become regular

Motor racing
Brand names of cigarettes and other products are displayed on Formula 1 cars and on billboards around the circuit.

smokers as those who were not interested in the sport. Motor racing is one of the few sports that are still allowed to use tobacco sponsorship, but there are plans within the EU to prevent all sponsorship of sports, including Formula 1 racing.

In the United States, tobacco advertisements are also banned from television. In 1998, 46 states signed the Master Settlement Agreement, which bans billboards and restricts outdoor advertising of cigarettes. Recent studies have shown that since 1999, the tobacco companies have dramatically increased their advertising spending in magazines read by large numbers of teenagers.

"Lured in large numbers by the glare and glamour of tobacco marketing that sells a deadly product as the taste of freedom and fashion, between 80,000 and 99,000 children and adolescents in the world take to tobacco every day." (Dr. Gro Harlem Brundtland, head of WHO Tobacco Free Initiative)

Advertising in the press and on posters and other forms of promotion are covered by voluntary agreements. The tobacco companies have agreed that their advertisements will not glamorize smoking or make it appeal to young people, and they will not link smoking with sporting success or make it sexually attractive. However, many people feel that some of the more obscure and puzzling advertisements have the effect of making smoking look very sophisticated. There are plans to tighten up the agreements, to restrict the promotion of tobacco at its point of sale in shops, to limit the advertising of tobacco brand names on non-tobacco goods such as boots, flip-flops, and baseball caps, and to prohibit the distribution of free cigarettes. Recently, there has been an increase in point-of-sale advertising in the United States, particularly in below-counter-level advertisements, which can be seen easily by young children.

Despite the increasing restrictions on tobacco advertising, the amount of money that tobacco companies spend on advertising and promotion has not decreased. The average amount spent each year is approximately $7 billion in the United States—that's a staggering $19 million per day —and $100 million in Great Britain.

A gentle cigarette
"Some people are known—and loved—for being gentle. So is this cigarette ... especially among our younger smokers" said this advertisement in the 1950s.

New Markets

Tobacco companies based in North America and Europe are seeing their home markets shrink. Both the number of smokers and the number of cigarettes smoked per smoker are falling as governments increase taxation on tobacco. Not surprisingly, these companies are turning their attention to the growing markets of East Asian countries, especially South Korea, Taiwan, and Japan. The advertising regulations in these countries are not as restrictive, and companies can use many techniques to persuade young people to start smoking. These campaigns can be very effective—tobacco advertisements are common along major roads, on the sides of buildings, and on television.

According to the World Health Organization (WHO), smoking rates among male Korean teenagers increased from 18 to 30 percent in the year following the entry of U.S. companies into the market. There was a fourfold increase in smoking among female teenagers. These increases were linked to the massive rise in tobacco advertising and promotion by both U.S. and Korean companies.

In developing countries, just under 50 percent of men but only 7 percent of women smoke. So tobacco companies are targeting women. In Sri Lanka, for example, a tobacco company sponsored a "Golden Tones Disco." It employed young women in shimmering golden saris to offer each young person entering the disco a free cigarette and lighter. Entry to the disco was free for women but men had to pay. Another brand was promoted by women driving around in sports cars handing out free cigarettes. In other countries, advertising campaigns aimed at women have included sponsored fashion collections. The new wave of marketing to women promotes cigarettes with perfumed scents and exotic flavors, and cigarettes with names that include the words "slims" and "lights." Product packaging and advertising have featured watercolors and pastels.

Campaign
In Tokyo, Japan, young women are employed to attract attention to cigarettes.

Smoking and Films

The amount of smoking that took place in films declined steadily during the 1960s–1980s, but there was an increase in the 1990s. The Dartmouth Medical School study in the United States looked at 603 films between 1988 and 1999 and gauged the level of smoking in each. Researchers then surveyed 5,500 school children at middle school in New Hampshire and Vermont to see if the films affected their smoking habits. The children surveyed were very aware of the smoking that took place in the films and could remember which actors were seen smoking. Those seen smoking most often were Leonardo DiCaprio, Tom Hanks, Julia Roberts, and Brad Pitt.

Why Do So Many Girls Smoke?

In the past, only a small percentage of girls smoked, but over the last decade this has changed and girls are fast catching up with boys. Teenage girls in Great Britain are the least likely of all groups to give up smoking.

So why do girls smoke? This can be summed up in one word: "image." Many of their role models, such as fashion models and pop stars, smoke and this can influence a young girl's decision to smoke. They understand the warnings on a pack of cigarettes, and realize that their clothes smell and that smoking gives them bad breath, but the lure of smoking is often too great. Their boyfriends may influence their smoking habits, and girls are more likely to start smoking if their boyfriends are smokers. Some boys like to see their

The big screen
Smoking is often glamorized in films.

girlfriends smoke. The effect is greater still if one or both of their parents smoke, and girls are especially influenced by an older brother.

As mentioned earlier, there are more female smokers in developed countries than in developing countries. Women in developed countries are more likely to be independent and to have careers, and they are more used to competing with men, especially the younger generations where attitudes associated with "girl power" are increasingly influential. These attitudes are seen in teenage girls too, as they compete with similar-aged boys at school. In contrast, women in developing countries are more likely to marry young and have to raise a large family.

Relationship
Girls may start smoking because their boyfriends do.

Saying no

I have never smoked—not even once. When I was at school several of my friends started smoking. We didn't all smoke, but the smokers kept passing around a pack of cigarettes. They told us that it felt so good to smoke—it gave you a kick, made you feel great. "Go on—try, it won't bite," they'd say. Some of their boyfriends smoked, too. When we went out together, they would sit at the other end of the table, puffing away, trying to look cool. Fortunately Carole, my best friend, didn't want to smoke either so we stuck it out together. After a while the smokers gave up and left us alone. I think they got bored trying to make us smoke. Now, when I look back, I am so pleased that we didn't give in. I don't think I missed much.
(Sophie, aged 25)

Smoking and Mobile Phones

There was an unexpected downturn in the number of teenage smokers in Great Britain during the late 1990s. Between 1996 and 1999, the number of 15-year-old smokers fell from 30 percent to 23 percent, a much faster decline than predicted. During the same period, mobile phone ownership increased, with a dramatic rise between 1999 and 2000. By August 2000, more than 70 percent of 15–17-year-olds owned a phone. Researchers have found that teenagers find mobile phones smart, chic, and adult. Teenagers can express their individuality through their choice of brand and model. Peer-group pressure has just as much effect on mobile phone ownership as it does on cigarette smoking. If one member of a group of friends has a mobile phone, then other members will see the phone as essential to socializing. Furthermore, the teenagers buy their phone cards in the same places as they would buy cigarettes. Since some teens cannot afford both, they have

Trends

Could the trend for mobile phones contribute to a decline in smoking?

to choose between having a mobile phone or smoking. Many teenagers feel that mobile phones, especially the newer models with WAP technology (giving internet access), create a more high-tech image than cigarettes, which are viewed as old technology. More research is currently under way to prove a link between the decline of smoking and the rise of the mobile phone, and research is needed in other parts of the world.

"Mobile phones are marketed in a very similar way to cigarettes with a subtle pitch that focuses on self-image, identity, and confidence. The mobile phone makers aren't doing anything wrong, but their advertising is very effective and seductive." (Anne Charlton, emeritus professor at the University of Manchester, England)

Selling to Children

To prevent children from buying cigarettes, many countries have laws that make it illegal for shopkeepers to sell cigarettes to young people. In Great Britain, the minimum age for buying tobacco is 16. In the United States, the majority of states have a minimum age of 18, with the exception of Alabama, Alaska, and Utah, which have a minimum age of 19, and Pennsylvania, which has a minimum age of 21. In both countries, shopkeepers can be prosecuted if they are found to have sold cigarettes to underage customers. Some U.S. states are applying penalties to children caught in possession of tobacco, as a means of discouraging under-age smoking. The penalties include carrying out a specific number of hours of community service and having your driving license suspended.

"I spend my spare time playing around with my computer. If I smoked I wouldn't have enough money to buy computer games and new equipment." (Mark, 14)

2 What's in a Cigarette?
The Main Ingredients

Cigarettes are made from tobacco. The tobacco leaves are harvested, dried, and transported to factories, where the tobacco is finely chopped and rolled up within a paper case, then cut to length. Different brands of cigarettes taste different, depending on the source of the tobacco, the amount of tar in the tobacco, and the additives that are mixed in with the tobacco by the cigarette manufacturers. The tobacco is blended for aroma, taste, and character to meet smokers' preferences.

Harvesting
Tobacco leaves being harvested on a plantation in Cuba.

Three types of tobacco are used in cigarettes: Virginia or flue-cured, burley, and oriental. Smokers' tastes vary considerably around the world. In Great Britain, people prefer the Virginia tobaccos, whereas in the United States, they prefer a blend of all three types of tobacco.

Nowadays, all cigarettes have filters that are located at the "mouth-end" of the cig-arette. The filter reduces the amount of smoke that reaches the smoker. Most

filters are made from cellulose fibers. The filter has no taste and is firm enough to hold its shape. Different kinds of filters deliver different amounts of tar and nicotine. The cigarette manufacturer can control the amount of air that enters the cigarette as it is smoked. This is called ventilation. A cigarette can be ventilated to dilute the smoke, which in turn reduces the amount of tar, nicotine, and carbon monoxide reaching the smoker. All cigarettes are ventilated by the paper, through which air can penetrate, and many are also ventilated through small air holes in the filter tip. When a smoker inhales, air is drawn in through these small holes and mixes with air drawn in through the lit end, diluting the smoke. Filter ventilation is a particularly important feature of lower-tar cigarettes.

What's in Smoke?

When a cigarette is lit, it starts to burn and releases smoke. When a smoker inhales, the smoke is drawn along the cigarette and through the filter, and from there into the mouth.

The smoke that enters the lungs of the smoker is called mainstream smoke. It is formed and inhaled when the smoker "puffs." Sidestream, or secondhand, smoke forms when the cigarette smolders between puffs. The smoker never inhales this smoke. As much as 85 percent of cigarette smoke in a room comes from secondhand smoke.

Tobacco contains approximately 2,500 different compounds. When it burns, many more are formed. Analysis indicates that there may be as many as 4,000 different chemical compounds in tobacco smoke, some of which have been proved to be harmful. Many potentially toxic gases are present in higher concentrations in secondhand smoke than in mainstream smoke.

Smokescreen
Sidestream smoke pollutes the atmosphere around a smoker.

The smoke contains tiny particles of tar (which is itself composed of many chemicals), nicotine, benzene and benzo(a)pyrene, as well as carbon monoxide, ammonia, dimethylnitrosamine, formaldehyde, and hydrogen cyanide in gaseous form. Some of these chemicals have irritant properties and 60 or so may be carcinogens, or cancer-forming substances. The effects of some of the main components of cigarette smoke are discussed below.

Radiation danger

Smoke also contains particles of a radioactive element called Polonium 210. Someone smoking 20 cigarettes a day gets a dose of radiation each year equivalent to about 200 chest X-rays.

Nicotine

Nicotine is the main compound present in tobacco. It is colorless but poisonous. In fact, nicotine has long been used as a pesticide to kill insects. If the nicotine content of one cigarette were injected straight into the body it would be fatal, but it is non-lethal if inhaled.

Nicotine is a powerful drug that can affect every organ in the body. It takes just seven seconds for the nicotine in cigarette smoke to reach the brain, where it causes the release of a chemical called dopamine. Dopamine creates pleasurable sensations and can change a person's mood. Nicotine has many effects on the body, but the most important one is to stimulate the release of the hormone adrenaline. This is often described as the "flight or fight" hormone. When you suddenly find yourself in a stressful situation, such as being frightened or being attacked by something or someone, adrenaline is released. It increases your heart rate and blood pressure and affects your nervous system, preparing you for running or fighting. You have probably noticed that if you are suddenly frightened your heart starts pounding—this is caused by adrenaline. The effects of adrenaline are the same, whether stimulated by a stress or by smoking.

"Smoking helps me to relax after a stressful day in the office. Within seconds of inhaling, I feel a sense of calm and I can unwind." (Alex, office worker)

Nicotine is addictive. Soon after smoking a cigarette, the brain starts to want more nicotine. Many people begin to feel increasingly uncomfortable until they have their next cigarette. Smoking feels pleasurable, but much of the pleasure of smoking is the relief from the withdrawal effects of nicotine. Many people feel distracted or unable to enjoy themselves when they are unable to smoke. One way to measure people's addiction to cigarettes is seeing if they need to smoke as soon as they wake up. In 1998, 31 percent of smokers had their first cigarette within 15 minutes of waking up. Young people who experiment with cigarettes quickly become addicted to the nicotine in tobacco, and they have similar levels of nicotine dependence as adults. Many teenagers who smoke light their first cigarette within 30 minutes of waking up.

It is the addiction to nicotine that makes it difficult, but not impossible, for people to stop smoking, and there are unpleasant withdrawal symptoms (see page 53).

Carbon Monoxide

Carbon monoxide is a deadly gas. It has no smell, and when it enters the bloodstream it can have serious effects. Normally, oxygen passes from the air in the lungs into the blood capillaries of the lungs. It is picked up by a molecule called hemoglobin, which is found in red blood cells. The red blood cells carry the oxygen to the tissues and organs of the body, where it is released. If carbon monoxide is present in the blood, red blood cells pick up this gas in preference to the oxygen. Therefore, less oxygen is carried by the red blood cells and less reaches the rest of the body. Having a small quantity of carbon monoxide in the blood can make a person feel tired and lacking in energy. In time, the regular presence of carbon monoxide in the blood leads to a thickening of the arteries, especially the coronary arteries supplying oxygen to the heart (see page 37).

Addiction
It is nicotine that makes a smoker light one cigarette after another, a practice referred to as "chain smoking."

The burning of gas in car engines also releases carbon monoxide, but modern cars are fitted with devices to remove this gas so the driver and passengers do not breathe it. There is no such device on a cigarette, although the filter could be designed to absorb carbon monoxide.

Tar

Tar is a sticky brown substance that is produced when tobacco is burned. It stains the fingers, teeth, and tongue of the smoker. It coats everything with which it comes into contact, especially the tiny hairs called *cilia* that line the trachea and bronchi (see page 33). Tar collects in the lungs and builds up over a number of years, staining the lung tissue. The presence of tar in the lungs is one of the main causes of lung cancer.

Hydrogen Cyanide

Tobacco smoke contains the gas hydrogen cyanide. This causes headaches, dizziness, weakness, nausea, vertigo, and stomachaches in both smokers and non-smokers.

Additives

A number of additives are mixed with tobacco during the manufacturing process. Before 1970, few additives were used in the manufacture of tobacco products; now more than 600 can be used. Manufacturers state that additives are used for a particular purpose. For example, food-type ingredients and flavorings can balance the natural tobacco taste, replace the sugars lost in the drying process, and give individual brands their characteristic flavor and aroma. Other additives have technological functions, such as controlling moisture, acting as preservatives, and serving as binders or fillers.

However, many anti-smoking groups claim that some additives have a different purpose: they are used to make the cigarette more addictive or more appealing to new smokers. Some additives enhance the addictive "kick" that

Tar

A health campaign poster showed this image of the amount of tar that collects in an average smoker's lungs.

smokers experience when they smoke the cigarette. For example, ammonium compounds affect cigarette smoke in a way that increases the amount of nicotine that is released. Some additives are used to enhance the taste of tobacco smoke to make the product more attractive to consumers. Sweeteners and chocolate may help to make cigarettes more enticing to first-time users. Chemicals such as eugenol and menthol soothe the throat, so smokers cannot feel the irritating effects of the smoke as it passes into their lungs. Cocoa may be used to dilate, or enlarge, the tubes into the lungs so that the smoke can pass more quickly and more deeply into the lungs. This enables more nicotine to pass into the bloodstream. Other additives mask the smell and visibility of secondhand smoke. This makes it less likely a non-smoker will complain about someone smoking in their vicinity.

There is considerable debate about the role of additives. Cigarette manufacturers dispute claims that additives are responsible for the increase in smoking. There are laws that control which additives may be used in manufacturing cigarettes. All the permitted additives must be tested for direct toxicity. This means the individual additive is tested to see if it has any toxic effect on humans. Unfortunately, when mixtures of additives are burned, new products of combustion are formed and these may be toxic. However, manufacturers are not required to state which additives they have used in their cigarettes. This means that smokers have no way of knowing whether the brand they smoke contains any or many additives.

A manufacturer's view

A statement from British American Tobacco says:

"Ingredients are not added to increase the amount of nicotine in cigarette smoke. Tobacco products are not "spiked" with nicotine. Ingredients do not make it easier for people to start smoking, or influence a decision to quit. Ingredients are not added to make cigarettes appealing to children, and there is no evidence whatsoever that they have this effect....sugars, cocoa, and fruit extracts...do not create a sweet, chocolate-like, or fruity taste in the smoke. They blend with tobacco, making a characteristic tobacco taste distinct from the effect these ingredients have in foods."

3 Smoking and Your Health
Effects on the Body

The first warning signs that smoking was harming people's health emerged in the 1930s when doctors noticed an increase in lung diseases such as emphysema and lung cancer. Since the 1950s, more than 70,000 scientific articles have shown that prolonged smoking causes premature death and disability. Today, smoking is still a major cause of death throughout the world.

A Worldwide Cause of Death
In the 50 years between 1950 and 2000, an estimated 66 million people worldwide died from tobacco-related diseases. The annual death rate is currently about 4 million, divided equally between developed and developing countries. Each year, approximately 500,000 people in the United States die prematurely as a result of smoking-related diseases. A similar number die in the 15 countries of the European Union, including more than 120,000 in Great Britain. In China, there are nearly 1 million deaths each year, a figure that is expected to double by 2025. Some scientists estimate that during the 21st century, the total number of deaths from a smoking-related cause could be as high as 1 billion. By 2030, smoking will probably be the single most likely cause of death in the world, causing about one in three of all adult deaths. More than two-thirds of these will be in the developing world.

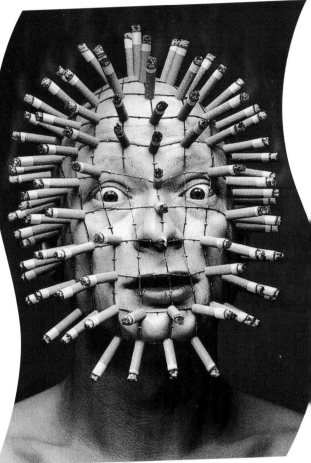

Dutch warning
A poster produced by the anti-smoking campaign in the Netherlands.

Lung cancer is probably the best-known disease that is linked to smoking. During the 1930s a number of doctors reported a rapid rise in lung cancer, which was once a rare disease, among smokers. In 1950, Sir Richard Doll, a leading cancer epidemiologist in Great Britain, published a paper that first established a link between smoking and lung cancer. Originally, he thought that the lung cancer was linked to the fumes produced by the increasing number of cars, but further analysis showed that tobacco was the culprit. However, smoking doesn't just cause lung cancer. It has been linked to many other diseases, such as bronchitis, coronary heart disease, and even blindness.

In countries where cigarette smoking has been common for several decades, the effects of smoking in people aged 35–69 accounts for:

- about 90 percent of all lung cancer cases
- 15 to 20 percent of other cancers
- 75 percent of chronic bronchitis and emphysema
- 25 percent of deaths from cardiovascular diseases.

In developing countries, smoking is more likely to cause chronic respiratory diseases than cancer and cardiovascular disease.

Increased risk

People who smoke are more likely than non-smokers to suffer from these conditions:

Severe circulatory disease
Angina (20 times the risk)
Peripheral vascular disease
Stomach and duodenal ulcers
Influenza
Pneumonia
Cataract (double the risk)
Loss of vision
Abnormal eye movements
Fungal eye infection
Macular degeneration (double the risk)
Acute necrotizing ulcerative gingivitis (gum disease) and tooth loss
Colon polyps
Crohn's disease (chronic inflamed bowel)
Osteoarthritis
Osteoporosis (in both sexes)
Depression
Tuberculosis
Hearing loss
Diabetes
Psoriasis (double the risk)
Skin wrinkling (double the risk)
Tendon and ligament injuries
Muscle injuries

Symptoms worse

The symptoms of the following are worse for smokers than non-smokers:

Asthma

Graves' disease (overactive thyroid gland)

Chronic rhinitis (chronic inflammation of the nose)

Multiple sclerosis

Diabetic retinopathy (eyes)

Optic neuritis (eyes)

Saying no

Remembering the physical problems that smoking can cause may make it easier to say no.

There is a wide range of little-publicized health problems associated with smoking. It can affect your senses of taste and smell. Smokers are more likely to develop facial wrinkles at a younger age and have dental hygiene problems. Stomach ulcers are made worse by smoking, and wounds, including surgical incisions, in smokers take longer to heal. Teenage smokers experience more asthma and respiratory symptoms than non-smokers, suffer poorer health, have more school absences, and are less fit.

Functions impaired

Smoking affects the following body functions:

Immune system (impaired)

Ejaculation (volume reduced)

Sperm count reduced

Sperm shape abnormalities increased

Sperm motility impaired

Sperm less able to penetrate the ovum

Menopause (onset 1.74 years early on average)

Fertility (30 percent lower in women who smoke)

Fitness
The pleasure of feeling and being fit is another argument for not smoking.

The immediate effects of smoking include:

- changes in blood vessels
- lower resistance to infection
- higher levels of carbon monoxide, leading to a lack of energy
- damage to the cilia lining the trachea and bronchial tubes, allowing more mucus, dirt, and germs to accumulate in the lungs
- bronchitis
- more frequent coughs, colds, earaches, sore throats, and other minor ailments.

"Jogging, swimming, and tennis help to keep us fit. Being fit is important to us. Exercise burns off the calories so we can eat more without worrying about putting on weight! We can't imagine what it must be like not to be fit." (Layla, Anna, and Stephanie, 14)

Smoking and Your Lungs

The first symptom of lung damage is the classic smoker's cough—an irritating cough that smokers experience first thing in the morning. It clears the lungs of accumulated mucus. As the damage gets worse, it may progress to more serious diseases, such as bronchitis, emphysema, and lung cancer.

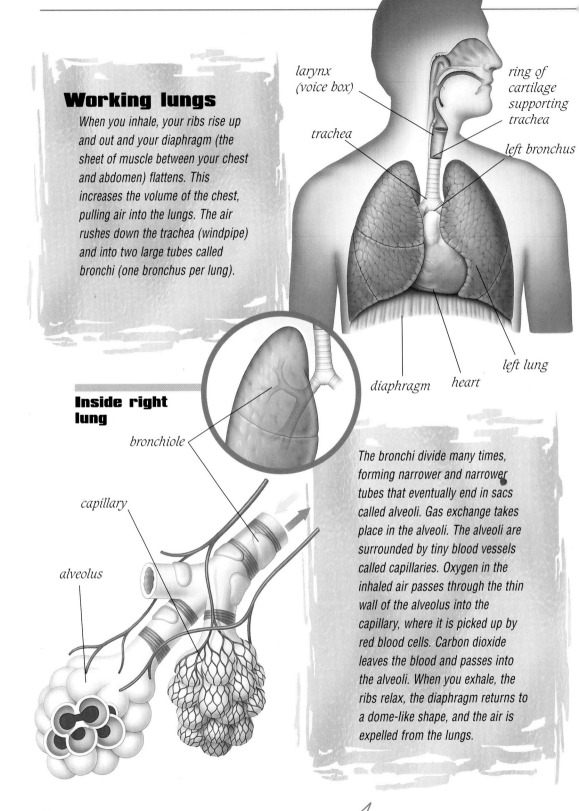

Working lungs

When you inhale, your ribs rise up and out and your diaphragm (the sheet of muscle between your chest and abdomen) flattens. This increases the volume of the chest, pulling air into the lungs. The air rushes down the trachea (windpipe) and into two large tubes called bronchi (one bronchus per lung).

larynx (voice box)

trachea

ring of cartilage supporting trachea

left bronchus

left lung

diaphragm

heart

Inside right lung

bronchiole

capillary

alveolus

The bronchi divide many times, forming narrower and narrower tubes that eventually end in sacs called alveoli. Gas exchange takes place in the alveoli. The alveoli are surrounded by tiny blood vessels called capillaries. Oxygen in the inhaled air passes through the thin wall of the alveolus into the capillary, where it is picked up by red blood cells. Carbon dioxide leaves the blood and passes into the alveoli. When you exhale, the ribs relax, the diaphragm returns to a dome-like shape, and the air is expelled from the lungs.

32

Inside Your Lungs

The trachea and the bronchi are lined with tiny hairs called cilia. The cilia are covered with a protective layer of mucus. Germs and dirt become trapped in the mucus, which is swept upwards by the cilia into the throat and swallowed. But the chemicals in tobacco smoke paralyze the cilia, allowing mucus to build up in the lungs. The presence of tar in the lungs stimulates the cells to produce even more mucus. A smoker has to cough to clear the mucus. The build-up of mucus can lead to bronchitis, a condition in which the trachea and bronchi become inflamed. The tubes swell up and breathing becomes difficult. Many people experience *acute* bronchitis when a cold or flu goes to the chest and they have a wheezy cough that clears up after a few days. Smokers suffer from *chronic* bronchitis, a progressive disease that kills thousands each year.

Emphysema

Emphysema is a long-term chronic condition affecting the lungs. Continual coughing damages the alveoli, and several sacs may join together. This means there are fewer, larger sacs and a reduced surface area of the lungs through which oxygen can be absorbed. The walls of the alveoli become less elastic, so they do not stretch and recoil as the lungs inflate and deflate. When exhaling, the lack of elasticity makes it difficult to force air from the lungs. Sufferers cannot oxygenate the body properly and they become breathless and exhausted after the slightest exercise. Unfortunately, there is no cure. Many sufferers ultimately become bedridden and have to use an oxygen tank to breathe.

Teaching with emphysema

I smoked 20 cigarettes a day for 20 years before quitting. I have emphysema now. My lungs are slowly getting worse. I can't sit in a smoky room because it affects my lungs. I find it difficult to take in enough breath to raise my voice so that pupils at the back can hear. It is very tiring to stand up and walk around a room for the duration of a lesson. Imagine having a strap around your chest and then trying to breathe in. You find you can't get enough air into your lungs—that's how I feel most of the time. Once we did a class experiment when pupils found out their lung capacity by blowing into a special bag. One or two of the pupils sang in the school choir and they had a really good lung capacity of 5 liters. Most had a lung capacity of about 4 liters. Mine was barely 2 liters. (John, teacher)

Lung Cancer

Lung cancer is the most common form of cancer in the world. Approximately 165,000 new cases were diagnosed in the United States in 2000, and in the same year more than 157,000 Americans died of the disease. In Great Britain, approximately 35,000 people die from the disease each year. Most of the new cases are people in their 60s and 70s who started smoking during and after World War II.

Fortunately, the number of deaths is beginning to decline as more people give up smoking. Fewer men are suffering from lung cancer, but now that there are more women smokers, an increasing number of women are diagnosed with this disease. In Europe and North America, more women die from lung cancer than from breast cancer.

Carcinogens

A large number of substances are known to cause cancers. They are called carcinogens. They include the tar in tobacco smoke, benzene, and even dietary supplements. Exposure to ultraviolet light, radioactivity, and X-rays can cause cells to become cancerous. Scientists believe that some people inherit genetic conditions that make them more vulnerable to certain kinds of cancer.

Cancer is an uncontrollable growth of cells. Something alters a cell's genes so that the cell divides over and over again, creating an irregular mass of cells called a tumor. By the time a tumor is detected there may be 1 billion cancerous cells present. The genes that cause the cancer are called oncogenes. These are genes that were once responsible for normal cell division but have been changed in some way so that they no longer function properly. Cancer cells live longer than other cells and disrupt the normal functioning of tissues and organs. Sometimes, a few cells break away from the main tumor and are carried in the bloodstream to other parts of the body to form secondary tumors. Many cancers are malignant, which means that they will spread and eventually kill the sufferer.

"It's not just older people who get lung cancer. I had to tell a 37-year-old man that he had lung cancer. He had a wife and two teenage children. He was devastated."
(Anthony, family doctor)

Lung cancer is difficult to detect in the early stages. It can take two years for a grape-sized clump of cancer cells to form. Most symptoms, such as a persistent cough, pains in the chest, breathlessness, and coughing up bloodstained mucus, only appear when the tumor is large enough to interfere with breathing. Unfortunately, some of these symptoms are similar to those that smokers may experience normally, so they ignore them. A large tumor can block a bronchus or a major bronchiole. This stops the air flowing into the lungs and causes blood vessels to bleed.

Most cancers are detected by an X-ray. On an X-ray film the tumor appears as a shadow in the chest cavity. Doctors may look inside the lungs using a tube called

Lung cancer

This colored X-ray shows an oval-shaped tumor in a person's left lung.

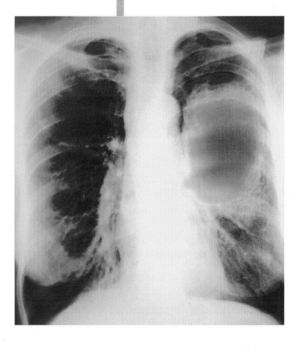

Surviving lung cancer

I was 49 when I was diagnosed with cancer in my right lung. The lung needed to be removed. Before operating on my lung, the surgeon removed some lymph nodes from my neck and carried out a biopsy to see if the cancer had spread. Well, it had. There was cancer in one lymph node. So he quickly closed me up. I was told I needed chemotherapy and radiation. I received three treatments of chemo over the next few months. It meant sitting for five hours while they pumped me full of the drug. I couldn't sleep for the first few days and I would hurt very badly for a day. And, of course, my hair fell out. They had to be careful when they gave me radiation, as the tumor was near my heart. Once my esophagus was burned and they had to squirt liquid painkiller down my throat just so that I could drink water. After 45 radiation treatments, I was sent for a scan which showed that the tumor had shrunk and there was no cancer anywhere else in my body. I had an operation to remove my right lung and all the surrounding lymph nodes. I was declared cancer-free. It was painful for a couple of months, but I kept getting better and regained my weight. At my 3-month check-up they did CAT scans, TBCs, and a liver function test, and found nothing.

an endoscope or examine the patient's chest using what is called a CT or CAT scan, which presents a very detailed image of the inside of the body. The cancer can be treated in a number of ways. Small cancers can be surgically removed. Sometimes a whole lung is removed to ensure a cure. Some patients receive radiotherapy, where strong X-rays are directed at the tumor to kill the cells. Chemotherapy makes use of powerful drugs to kill the cancerous cells. Despite all the advances in cancer treatments, 75 percent of all people diagnosed with lung cancer die of the disease, with fewer than 10 percent of patients surviving five years after diagnosis. This is because the cancer spreads through the bloodstream before the first tumor is even detected.

Overall, up to 20 percent of all cancer deaths can be linked to smoking. Smoking is connected with cancers of the mouth, lip, throat, stomach, pancreas, bladder, kidney, liver, and cervix as well as leukemia (a cancer that affects the white blood cells).

The Risks

The risk of contracting lung cancer depends on how many cigarettes are smoked each day and over how many years.

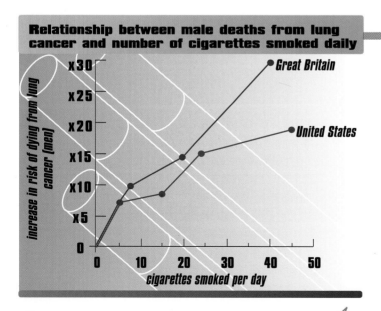

Relationship between male deaths from lung cancer and number of cigarettes smoked daily

increase in risk of dying from lung cancer (men)

● Great Britain

● United States

cigarettes smoked per day

Smoking and lung cancer
The more cigarettes a person smokes, the greater his or her risk of death from lung cancer.

A person who smokes 1 to 14 cigarettes each day has eight times the risk of dying from lung cancer than a non-smoker; a person who smokes more than 25 cigarettes each day has 15 times more risk. The number of years that a person has been a smoker is even more important than the number of cigarettes. The longer a person smokes, the greater is the risk of getting lung cancer. For example, smoking one pack of cigarettes per day for 40 years increases the risk of lung cancer by eight times compared with smoking two packs per day for 20 years. Approximately 16 percent of men who smoke throughout their adult life until they are 75 years old will get lung cancer—that's if another smoking-related disease, such as heart disease, doesn't kill them first. However, the risk of contracting lung cancer starts to decrease as soon as the person gives up smoking.

The incidence of lung cancer is also linked to social class. For example, men in the 15 to 64 age group who are manual and factory workers are three times as likely to contract lung cancer as professional men.

Smoking and the Blood Circulation

Coronary heart disease is a leading cause of death in most developed countries, and about one-quarter of these deaths can be linked to smoking. Smoking increases the risk of having a heart attack by two or three times.

As a person gets older, fatty deposits form patches on the lining of major arteries. The deposits become more frequent and larger. Some patches may

Coronary blood vessels

aorta (major artery)

pulmonary artery to lungs

main vein from head

pulmonary veins from lungs

coronary artery

main vein from body

heart muscle

join together and cause an artery to become narrower, which restricts the blood flow along the artery. The heart has to pump harder to get the blood through. However, there are no symptoms until a major artery is affected.

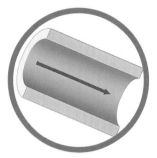

blood flow through normal artery

The coronary arteries supply the heart muscle with oxygenated blood. Any blockage in these arteries would reduce the supply of oxygenated blood to the heart. Sometimes, the surface of the fatty deposits becomes rough and this causes a blood clot, or thrombus, to form. If this occurs in a coronary artery, the clot blocks the artery completely, starving the heart of oxygen and causing a heart attack. Unless the person gets medical treatment straight away, he or she is likely to die. A person may get an early warning when the coronary arteries become partially blocked. He or she may suffer from chest pains during or after exercise. This condition is

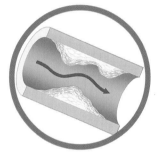

blood flow through artery with fatty deposits

Having a heart attack

David was driving to work when he felt dizzy and had a twinge of pain in his chest. He pulled to the side of the road and got out of his car. He started to sweat heavily and found he could not swallow. The pain spread across his chest and down his left arm. He was having a heart attack. He flagged down a passing driver who called for an ambulance. After his arrival at the hospital, David was attached to an electrocardiogram to monitor his heart and given a diamorphine injection to relieve the pain. He was also given an injection of a "clot-busting" drug. This type of drug breaks down the clot that has formed in the arteries, allowing more blood to flow through. If given soon after the onset of the heart attack, it can save a person's life. He had some blood tests and an X-ray. David spent a week in hospital before being allowed home. He was given medicine to reduce the likelihood of another attack and told to take aspirin, which helps to prevent the clots from re-forming. It was 12 weeks before he was fit enough to return to work. He is now on the road to recovery. He has stopped smoking and changed his diet.

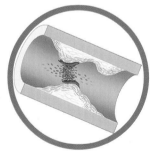

formation of blood clot

called angina. Angina can be treated, but it is a warning that the person is at risk from a heart attack. A person with blocked coronary arteries can have coronary bypass surgery. This is when the blocked section of a coronary artery is replaced by a length of vein taken from the patient's leg.

The incidence of heart disease has increased dramatically over the last 50 years, suggesting that the causes of the disease are linked to lifestyle. The main factors are fatty diets, stress, lack of exercise, and smoking. The nicotine and carbon monoxide from smoke increase the tendency of blood to clot and this adds to the blockage in the arteries. The carbon monoxide increases the rate at which the fatty deposits are laid down.

It's not just the heart that can be affected by smoking. The blood vessels of the legs and arms, known as the peripheral circulation, can also be harmed. One unpleasant condition is peripheral vascular disease, which can result in the amputation of one or both legs. The arteries supplying the arms and legs become narrower as fatty deposits build up. The person experiences leg pain in the calf muscles when walking or taking exercise. As the arteries become narrower, the pain gets worse. Eventually, there is so little blood flow to the leg that the skin and other tissues die and gangrene, a type of infection, sets in. Doctors have to amputate the leg to prevent the infection from spreading and becoming life-threatening. Smoking causes approximately 90 percent of cases of peripheral vascular disease. In Great Britain, there are about 2,000 amputations each year.

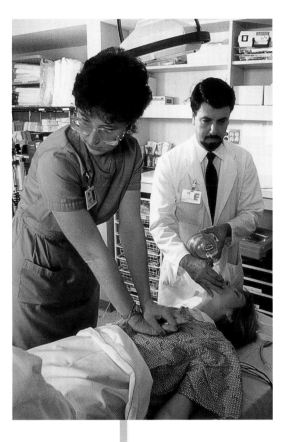

Heart attack
Cardiac massage and giving oxygen through a face mask are two life-saving treatments.

Strokes

If the blood flow through the arteries supplying the brain is restricted, part of the brain can become starved of oxygen. This causes the brain cells to die and the person is said to have had a stroke. This can result in loss of function or sensation associated with the part of the brain that was starved of oxygen. Smoking causes an increase in blood pressure and this increases the risk of a stroke.

Smoking and the Reproductive Organs

Smoking can affect sperm production in men and menstruation in women. Smoking in men has been associated with a reduced sperm count, increased sperm abnormalities, and impotence (an inability to have an erection because of decreased blood flow to the penis). Smoking in women has been linked to an increased likelihood of menstrual problems and an earlier menopause (the end of a woman's menstrual cycles). On average, women smokers go through menopause up to two years earlier than non-smokers and have a greater risk of developing osteoporosis (see page 41).

The most common and reliable form of contraception is various forms of "the pill," which is taken daily for 21 days each month. Each pill contains a dose of female reproductive hormones that is sufficient to prevent the woman from ovulating and becoming pregnant. One of the side effects of the contraceptive pill, especially if taken over a long time, is an increased risk of a heart attack, stroke, or other cardiovascular disease. If a woman smokes as well, the risk is 10 times greater than for a non-smoking woman who takes the pill.

Smoking and Your Skin

For most people, looking good is important. But smoking can have long-term effects on the skin and cause premature aging. The smoke damages the skin's structure by destroying

Tar stains
Besides affecting the texture of the skin, smoking gradually stains the hand that holds the cigarettes.

the collagen, one of the structural components in skin. The collagen fibers give support to the skin and keep it firm. When collagen is damaged, the skin loses its elasticity and becomes leathery. The result is wrinkles, especially around the eyes and mouth. The tar in cigarette smoke often gives the complexion an ash-grey color. By the time a regular smoker reaches the age of 40, their skin condition is more like that of someone 20 years older.

Smoking and Osteoporosis

Osteoporosis is a disease that affects older people, especially women. The slow loss of bone density, which results from a shortage of the mineral calcium, causes the bones to become brittle. When an older women falls, osteoporosis makes it more likely that she will fracture her hip. Although a hip fracture can be repaired, it can cause some degree of disability. Researchers have found that the bones of smokers lose calcium at a greater rate than the bones of non-smokers. Consequently, as many as one in every eight hip fractures could be the result of smoking.

"I can't believe the number of models who smoke. They spend a fortune on skin products and then they ruin it all by smoking. Don't they realize what they are doing to their skin? By the time they are 30 their face will be too wrinkled for this business."(Rachel, make-up artist)

Health Warnings

In 1966, the U.S. government passed laws requiring cigarette manufacturers to place this warning on all of their cigarette packs: "Caution: smoking may be hazardous to health." This has appeared on all advertising since 1972. Over the years the warning has changed, and now there are several different phrases that manufacturers must use.

The EU requires the manufacturer to place a general warning "Tobacco seriously damages health" on the most visible surface of a cigarette pack, together with a second warning on the next largest surface. This could be any one of the following:

- "Smoking causes cancer"
- "Smoking causes heart disease"
- "Smoking causes fatal diseases"

- "Smoking kills"
- "Smoking can kill"
- "Smoking when pregnant harms your baby"
- "Protect children: don't make them breathe your smoke"
- "Smoking damages the health of those around you"
- "Stopping smoking reduces the risk of serious disease"
- "Smoking causes cancer, chronic bronchitis, and other chest diseases"
- "More than (…) people die each year in (name of country) from lung cancer"
- "Every year, (…) people are killed in road accidents in (name of country)—(…) times more die from their addiction to smoking"
- "Every year, addiction to smoking claims more victims than road accidents"
- "Smokers die younger"
- "Don't smoke if you want to stay healthy"
- "Save money: stop smoking"

Plans are in place in the EU to limit the tar, nicotine, and carbon monoxide content of a cigarette to 10 mg tar, 1 mg nicotine, and 10 mg carbon monoxide. It is also proposed that these regulations should apply to cigarettes made for export as well as those sold within the EU.

The strongest messages are seen on cigarette packs sold in Canada. Since December 2000, cigarette manufacturers have had to print one of 16 new health warnings. Each of these is accompanied by a graphic image, for example, "Cigarettes cause mouth diseases" followed by "Cigarette smoke causes oral cancer, gum diseases, and tooth loss," with a photo of a smoker's open mouth and teeth.

Health warnings
These are four of the images printed on cigarette packs in Canada to warn people about the results of smoking.

Lawsuits

In recent years there have been a number of court cases, particularly in the United States, where smokers with lung cancer and other smoking-related diseases have sued the tobacco companies for damages. As the number of people suffering from these diseases increases, so do the medical costs to health services. In November 1998, the tobacco industry agreed to pay 50 states in the United States a total of $246 billion over a number of years. This is to compensate for the billions of taxpayers' dollars spent on treating smoking-related illnesses. Now the states are deciding how to spend this money.

Class action suits

In July 2000, a court case in Florida made legal history. A jury ordered five of the world's largest tobacco companies to pay an unprecedented $145 billion in damages for harming thousands of smokers living in Florida. This was also the first successful "class action suit" in which the case was fought on behalf of thousands of unidentified people rather than named individuals. As expected, the case has been appealed, and it is likely that the ruling will be overturned. If it is not, each of the 700,000 smokers in Florida would have to go to court to make their own claim for a share of the damages, so the case could go on for decades. Class actions in 28 other states have failed, mainly because smoking was considered to be the responsibility of the individual.

A case lost

Norwegian Robert Lund (right) shakes hands with the head of Tiedemanns tobacco company before a newsworthy court case in 2000. Lund had lung cancer and sued the company for not warning him of the dangers of smoking and for causing his illness. Lund (a smoker since the 1950s) died before the end of the case. The court ruled against him, saying that tobacco's addictiveness did not free him from responsibility: he had continued to smoke even after the dangers had become widely known and accepted. His family said they would appeal.

4 Passive Smoking
Cigarettes and Non-Smokers

Passive smoking is the inhaling of other people's smoke. A non-smoker sitting beside a smoker breathes in both the secondhand smoke from the burning tip of the cigarette and the mainstream smoke that has been inhaled and then exhaled by the smoker. In fact, the smoke released from the lit end of a cigarette often contains greater amounts of nicotine and carbon monoxide than the smoke that is inhaled by the smoker, since it has not passed through a filter. Not surprisingly, non-smokers are concerned that breathing in other people's smoke could be harmful to their health.

No choice
This child in Bangladesh cannot help breathing in secondhand smoke.

Health Risks

Some of the immediate effects of passive smoking include eye irritation, headache, cough, sore throat, dizziness, and nausea. Anyone who suffers from asthma can experience a significant reduction in their lung function when they are exposed to smoke, and new cases of asthma may be induced in children whose parents smoke.

In the longer term, passive smokers suffer an increased risk of a range of smoking-related diseases. Smoking causes most cases of lung cancer, but a small percentage have been linked to passive smoking. For example, non-smokers who are exposed to passive smoking in the home have as much as a 25 percent increased risk of heart disease and lung cancer. About 600 non-smokers die from lung cancer each year in Great Britain and about 3,000 in the United States. One of the best-known cases involved an entertainer, Roy Castle, a lifelong non-smoker who died from lung cancer. He attributed his cancer to years of working in clubs where smoking was permitted.

Entertainment
Roy Castle blamed his lung cancer on the smoky atmosphere of jazz clubs, where he used to play. Before he died, he worked hard to publicize the dangers of smoking.

The U.S. Environmental Protection Agency has been studying the risks of passive smoking compared with other carcinogens in the environment. It found that the lifelong risk from passive smoking was more than 100 times higher than the estimated effect of 20 years of exposure to asbestos, a carcinogen found in old buildings.

There have been numerous studies about the link between passive smoking and lung cancer, but the number of cases involved was fairly low. In 1998, the widely differing results of two large studies were published. The WHO's International Agency for Research on Cancer (IARC) found little or no increased risk of lung cancer from exposure to tobacco smoke in the home, at

work, in vehicles, or in indoor public settings, such as restaurants. In contrast, the SCOTH report (Report of the Scientific Committee on Tobacco and Health, Great Britain) concluded that for people with long-term exposure to environmental tobacco smoke the increased risk of lung cancer was about 20 to 30 percent.

Asthma
A child who lives with smokers is twice as likely to develop asthma.

Smoking in the Home

Despite the arguments about the link between smoking and lung cancer, most doctors agree that environmental tobacco smoke has harmful effects on children. Children living with parents who smoke have been found to be less healthy than children living in smoke-free homes.

Children who live in smoking households are more likely to suffer from a number of respiratory diseases, such as bronchitis and pneumonia. A study in 1999 by the International Consultation on Environmental Tobacco Smoke and Child Health found that in households where both parents smoke, young children have a 72 percent increased risk of respiratory illnesses. Children in smoking homes have twice the risk of developing asthma and they suffer from more coughs and colds. These children also receive an amount of nicotine equivalent to smoking 80 cigarettes per year.

The risks of parental smoking on children include:

- Sudden Infant Death Syndrome (25 percent linked to smoking)
- 30 percent greater likelihood of developing middle ear disease, the most common cause of deafness in children

- increased incidence of asthma
- poor lung function
- more coughs and colds
- greater likelihood of being admitted to hospital for bronchitis and pneumonia in the first year of life
- development of respiratory disease in adult life.

"I didn't think smoking once in a while would hurt my baby. But when I went for a prenatal check-up the nurse told me about the dangers of smoking while pregnant. I stopped right away." (Gloria)

Harm to the Unborn Child

The presence of nicotine, carbon monoxide, and tar in the body of a pregnant woman can damage the development of her unborn child. Smoking during pregnancy results in babies with a lower than average birth weight. Babies who were exposed before birth to their mother's cigarette smoke have been found to grow up with reduced lung function and an air flow to their lungs that is up to 6 percent below normal. Studies in California showed that children born to women who smoked 10 or more cigarettes a day after the fourth month of pregnancy made poorer progress at school up to the age of 16.

Despite the health warnings displayed in clinics and doctor's offices, many women still smoke during their pregnancy. In Great Britain, 23 percent of women smoke throughout their pregnancy, and a further 33 percent smoke at some point during their pregnancy. Furthermore, only a small number of men give up smoking when their partners become pregnant.

In pregnant women, smoking leads to an increased risk of:

- spontaneous abortion (miscarriage)
- bleeding during pregnancy
- premature birth
- low birth weight (which is associated with greater risks of ill-health and failure to thrive)
- Sudden Infant Death Syndrome

No Smoking Areas

Increasingly, public buildings, offices, schools, hospitals, and transport systems in Europe, North America, parts of Southeast Asia, and Australia are becoming no-smoking zones. In Singapore and parts of California, it is illegal to smoke anywhere in public, including outdoors. These laws are to protect the non-smoking public from the harmful effects of passive smoking. In contrast, there are few, if any, controls in Eastern Europe, many Asian and African countries, and Central and South America.

Banned
Smokers gather outside their non-smoking workplace.

Some of these controls have come through government legislation. For example, in 1988, Great Britain's Independent Scientific Committee on Smoking and Health recommended that non-smoking should be regarded as the norm in enclosed areas used by the public or employees and special provision should be made for smokers, rather than vice versa.

Consumer pressure is forcing rapid change in restaurants, movie theaters, and leisure facilities. Studies of the economic impact of introducing no-smoking areas in restaurants show that the majority of customers think these are a good idea. Most public transport systems are smoke-free, as are many planes. Pressure from non-smokers has persuaded many airline companies to offer no-smoking flights, even on journeys of six or more hours.

No smoking

In Taiwan, smoking has been banned since 1997 in all public areas, including airplanes and hotels.

A smoke-free office

I don't smoke, so I really objected to people in my office lighting up at their desks. Despite air conditioning, the air was still smoky. I had to breathe their smoke whether I liked it or not. I went home each night with a headache and smoky clothes that had to go straight to the laundry. The smoke was affecting my health. A chain smoker joined the team and things were so bad that the non-smokers made an official complaint to the management. Now the office has been made "no smoking" throughout and the smokers have to leave the building if they want a cigarette.
(Liam, accounts manager)

5 Kicking the Habit
How to Stop Smoking and Stay Stopped

Many adult smokers say that they know about the risks of smoking—the effect on their health, the smells, the cost, even the inconvenience of having to smoke outside the back door at home or at work. They don't want to give it up because they are addicted to nicotine. Beating the addiction is the key to giving up smoking successfully.

Persuading young people to give up smoking is even more difficult. One of the problems with smoking is that the effects are long-term. The damage builds up over a number of years. There are a few early-warning signs, such as the early-morning cough and shortness of breath, but these are often ignored, or considered to be one of the "downsides," or hazards, of smoking. Today, many young people are unfit as a result of their sedentary lifestyles—sitting in front of the TV or computer and being driven in the car—so perhaps they don't notice that their lung capacity is a fraction of what it should be. A long and painful death from lung cancer seems remote to a 15-year-old, so it is unlikely that teenagers worry very much that smoking has been called a form of "slow-motion suicide."

Giving up
It is easier to give up smoking completely than to try to reduce your smoking gradually.

There are various ways of kicking the smoking habit. Whichever way is chosen, the effect on health is almost immediate. Within days, the ex-smoker will have fewer coughs, cleaner clothes, and easier breathing. Lung capacity improves and the ex-smoker will soon feel better physically. The risk of heart disease decreases too, especially during the first year.

One of the most difficult aspects of giving up smoking is beating the nicotine addiction. Giving up this drug is difficult and the person will suffer from withdrawal symptoms, such as irritability and restlessness. Fortunately, these effects disappear after a few weeks.

Help Yourself to Quit

People may tell you that it is easier to cut down on the number of cigarettes you smoke each day than to make a clean break. Although this might seem a good idea, it is difficult to do. One common response to cutting down is that the smoker smokes more of each cigarette. Though he or she is smoking a fewer number of cigarettes, they may actually be smoking just as much in terms of the substances ingested. And any amount of smoking exposes the smoker to nicotine.

There are four phases to giving up cigarettes:

⦾ thinking about stopping
⦾ preparing to stop
⦾ stopping
⦾ staying stopped.

Thinking About Stopping

One of the keys to success is really wanting to stop, and willpower has a tremendous role to play. So before you stop, think about the benefits of stopping—a healthier body and a longer life, fresher breath, and smoke-free clothes. Work out how much money you will save and plan how to spend it.

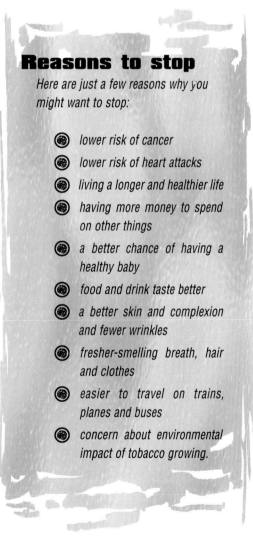

Reasons to stop

Here are just a few reasons why you might want to stop:

⦾ *lower risk of cancer*
⦾ *lower risk of heart attacks*
⦾ *living a longer and healthier life*
⦾ *having more money to spend on other things*
⦾ *a better chance of having a healthy baby*
⦾ *food and drink taste better*
⦾ *a better skin and complexion and fewer wrinkles*
⦾ *fresher-smelling breath, hair and clothes*
⦾ *easier to travel on trains, planes and buses*
⦾ *concern about environmental impact of tobacco growing.*

"I'm going to stop smoking on
my birthday. That's in two weeks time.
My girlfriend is determined to make sure I stop.
She's arranged for me to go to the game with
a few friends and then we're going out for
dinner followed by a late movie, so she
can keep a close eye on me!"
(James, 19)

Stay busy

Make sure you keep busy all day so you have no time to think about that cigarette!

Preparing to Stop

For many people, smoking is a habit that is linked to certain times of day, certain places, and friends. It's important to break as many of these links as possible. So before you actually stop, think about when and where you smoke. These times and places are danger spots. Work out in advance how to avoid situations where you instinctively want a cigarette, and how to avoid the company of other smokers and places where you will be tempted to smoke or can buy cigarettes. Sometimes it helps to occupy your day with a new activity. This will prevent you thinking about smoking. Try to get help from family and friends. Tell them you are stopping so that they can offer support and encouragement. Make sure you can call a friend if you feel like smoking so he or she can talk you through it. Most likely, it will be the most difficult not to smoke during stressful times.

Stopping

Choose a day to stop completely. Make sure the chosen day will not be too stressful. Then get rid of all your cigarettes, ashtrays, and lighters. The first day will be important. Make sure you have plenty to do. You could get up late and have a long relaxing bath, go for a long walk, or play some sports. It's just as important to plan a treat for yourself at the end of the day. Don't sit around thinking about smoking—keep busy and distract yourself. Keep reminding yourself that just because you want a cigarette it doesn't mean you have to have one.

It's now that the first signs of nicotine withdrawal will make themselves known. You may feel restless, irritable, unable to concentrate, unable to sleep, and accident-prone. You may experience mood swings, feeling happy one minute and depressed the next. But don't give in—these things will pass and you will quickly start to feel the benefits.

Staying Stopped

Take it a day at a time. Each day try to stop for one more day. Think positively. If you are offered a cigarette say, "No thanks, I don't smoke." Give yourself lots to do—clean your bedroom, do the laundry, go to places where smoking is not allowed, take up a new sport, or start jogging. During the first week, you will start to feel the benefits of not smoking but you may experience a bad cough. This is the first phase of cleaning out your lungs. You may miss the calming effects of a cigarette, so learn to relax. You can learn techniques that help you to relax naturally, such as meditation and yoga.

Don't let yourself be fooled into thinking one cigarette won't hurt—it will. After one, you'll want another and another. A clean break, or going "cold turkey," is best. Keep reminding yourself of all the health benefits and the fact that you won't want to go through "giving up" again.

Yoga
Some people find yoga a good way to help them relax.

"I have often been tempted to start again. It has been hard. I still tell myself that staying off the cigs is like a game of chutes and ladders. Just one drag on a cigarette would send me down the longest chute right back to square one. And there's no way I want to go back and do it all again."
(Maxine, ex-smoker)

Giving up

The first day was just terrible and it seemed as if it lasted forever. I had picked a Saturday as my stop-smoking day. I got up and the very first thing I thought about was a cigarette. It's not normally like that but maybe because I knew I couldn't have a cigarette I couldn't get it out of my mind. I went shopping with a friend. It's amazing just how many stores sell cigarettes—they kept jumping out at me. Every time I stopped to look, my friend would drag me past. I didn't feel great and was I in a bad mood! I yelled at everybody. I was supposed to go out with friends for the evening but I couldn't face being nice to them so I stayed in. I tried watching television. I wandered around the apartment, tried reading some magazines, but I couldn't concentrate. Then I listened to a couple of CDs. Great—it was finally time for bed but I couldn't get to sleep. As I lay in bed all I could think of was cigarettes. Finally I fell asleep but I didn't feel much better when I woke up. The second day was just as bad. So was the third day, but at least I was in college for the day and had lectures to go to. I don't know exactly when I stopped thinking about cigarettes. I suddenly realized that I hadn't thought about a cigarette all afternoon. The first week was the worst. After about four days I started to cough—that was disgusting. Far worse than any morning cough I had had before. By the next weekend, things were better. I went to see a movie with some friends, which was good because the theater was non-smoking. Looking back I can't believe I stuck it out. But I did and I definitely don't want to go through that again—ever.
(Sandra, ex-smoker)

Giving up smoking can be tough and requires a tremendous amount of willpower. Most people find the first few days difficult and for some it can be a long struggle, but things will usually start to get better after the third or fourth day. Many people will not succeed the first time. Don't worry. You can always try again.

Nicotine-Replacement Therapies

If willpower alone does not work and you can't beat the addiction, you can use nicotine chewing gum, lozenges, inhalers, or nicotine patches to help stop the craving for the drug. The chances of successfully giving up smoking are doubled by using nicotine replacement therapies. These allow the ex-smoker to come off nicotine gradually by using a low dose of the drug to take the edge off the craving and give a "soft landing." The transdermal nicotine patch is like a sticky plaster and is worn on the upper arm during the day. It releases a steady stream of nicotine into the blood. The nicotine inhaler is a hand-held device designed to overcome the physical craving for nicotine and the behavioral dependence of handling cigarettes. Some lozenges, capsules, and tablets contain small doses of nicotine and aim to reduce the craving; others contain silver acetate, which produces an unpleasant taste when a cigarette is smoked. Unfortunately, few of these products have been clinically tested, but they have been found to help many people.

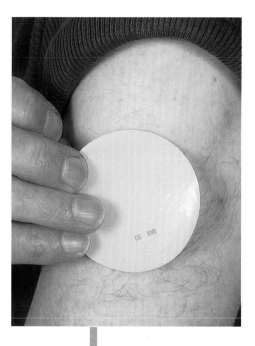

Patch
A nicotine patch slowly releases nicotine through the skin and into the bloodstream.

Zyban

In 1997 a new anti-smoking treatment became available. It is a little-known anti-depressant called bupropion, with the trade name Zyban—a drug that reduces the craving for nicotine. It is the first quitting aid that is not based on substituting nicotine in tobacco with another form of nicotine. Zyban is available only on prescription. First the patient takes the drug twice daily for two weeks while he or she's still smoking. Then stops smoking but continues to take the drug for another 12 weeks.

Zyban is an anti-depressant that works directly in the brain. It disrupts the addictive nature of nicotine by affecting the same chemical messengers. One of the pleasurable effects of nicotine is its release of dopamine from brain cells. Smoking floods the brain with dopamine. Zyban causes the release of dopamine, but in much smaller quantities. This treatment seems to be more successful than the nicotine replacement therapies but as always there is an element of willpower involved. Zyban can also be used with nicotine-replacement aids to increase further the chances of quitting.

"I've been a smoker for 36 years and have been through things you wouldn't believe, trying to stop. But Zyban seems to be a miracle! I can handle cravings— they're more like thoughts about a cigarette, really. Real cravings have been few." (Gail)

Getting Help

If you find you still can't stop, there are many professional and self-help groups that can offer help and support. Your doctor, pharmacist, or health professional should be able to give advice and tell you if there are special services for smokers in your area. Some people try hypnosis, acupuncture, aversion therapy and relaxation classes. There is little evidence to support the effectiveness of either acupuncture or hypnosis as a means of stopping smoking, but some smokers have found such methods to be useful.

Herbal cigarettes

Some people turn to herbal cigarettes, but these can cause just as many problems as tobacco. Herbal cigarettes produce tar and carbon monoxide, and some brands have a tar content equivalent to tobacco cigarettes. Furthermore, the use of herbal cigarettes reinforces the habit of smoking which smokers need to overcome.

Weight Watching

Many people, especially women, worry about putting on weight when they stop smoking. Nicotine changes the appetite and increases the body's metabolism, so that it burns up more energy. As a result, four in every five smokers gain weight when they stop smoking. The average weight gain is about 4.4 pounds (2 kg), but this can be lost in a couple of weeks once the person has finally stopped smoking. For example, changing the diet, avoiding alcohol, and taking more exercise will increase the chances of not gaining too much weight. The rapid improvement in lung function will also help make exercise that much easier.

National Campaigns

Many governments and organizations, such as the WHO (World Health Organization), sponsor campaigns to persuade people to stop smoking. These may take the form of advertisements on TV and in national newspapers and campaigns in schools. There have even been TV programs to help people give up, with ordinary people appearing on them each week. These programs form a type of national support group, and there are books, pamphlets, and websites to accompany them.

Examples
A billboard located in Times Square, New York City, shows famous athletes and entertainers who do not smoke.

In Great Britain, there is an annual No Smoking Day. In the United States, the America Cancer Society organizes the "Great American Smoke-Out," which aims to get as many of the 48 million smokers as possible to stop for the day. There is also a "Kick Butts Day" on April 4, which is aimed at stopping children from smoking. The WHO organizes the World No

Tobacco Day on May 31. Many people find a no-smoking day to be a good idea to help people stop smoking since they will not be alone in trying to give up on that day.

Beneficial health changes when you stop smoking

TIME SINCE QUITTING	BENEFICIAL HEALTH CHANGES
20 minutes	Blood pressure and pulse rate return to normal.
8 hours	Nicotine and carbon monoxide levels in blood fall by 50 percent and oxygen levels return to normal.
24 hours	No more carbon monoxide in the body. Lungs start to clear out mucus and other smoking debris.
48 hours	No nicotine left in the body. Senses of taste and smell are greatly improved.
72 hours	Breathing becomes easier and energy levels increase.
2-12 weeks	Circulation improves.
3-9 months	Fewer coughs, wheezes, and breathing problems. Lung function is increased by up to 10 percent.
5 years	Risk of a heart attack falls to about half that of a smoker.
10 years	Risk of lung cancer falls to half that of a smoker. Risk of heart attack falls to the same as someone who has never smoked.

"It's easier not to start than it is to stop"

Christy Turlington, a well-known model, was a heavy smoker for many years before she finally managed to quit. In 1997, her father died of lung cancer. Since then she has become actively involved in a campaign to educate teenagers about tobacco addiction. In a 30-second television commercial in which she tells viewers how she quit smoking and lost her father to lung cancer, Christy says:

"In my life, there are two people in my family who have quit smoking. Me and my Dad. For me it took seven years. Nothing worked. When I finally did quit for good, I knew it was one of the biggest accomplishments of my life. My Dad, it was different for him. He stopped December 1996, just six months before he died from lung cancer."

Resources

Books

Engelmann, Jeanne and Gladys Folkers. *Taking Charge of My Mind and Body: A Girl's Guide to Outsmarting Alcohol, Drugs, Smoking, and Eating Problems.* Minneapolis: Free Spirit Publishing, 1997.

Hyde, Margaret O. *Know About Smoking.* New York: McGraw-Hill, 1995.

Kevishan, Elizabeth. *Everything You Need to Know About Smoking.* New York: Rosen Publishing Group, Inc., 2000.

Lange, Susan L. and Beth M. Marks. *Teens & Tobacco: A Fatal Attraction.* Breckenridge, CO: Twenty-First Century Books, 1996.

Pringle, Laurence P. *Smoking: A Risky Business.* New York: William Morrow & Company, 1996.

Williams, Mary E. (ed.) *Teen Smoking (Contemporary Issues Companion).* San Diego: Greenhaven Press, 2000.

Videos

SLAM

A 15-minute video produced by the Center for Disease Control and Prevention's Office on Smoking and Health. It tells the story of Leslie Nuchow, a talented but unsigned young singer-songwriter, who refused to have her music associated with a cigarette-marketing campaign targeted at young people. The video helps young people be more aware of the power and persuasiveness of cigarette advertising and to explore ways to resist the influences of the tobacco industry.

Websites

http://www.pbs.org/inthemix/shows/show_smoking.html
Learn about the hazards and dangers of smoking with PBS's In The Mix teen hosts. This web site also includes interviews with health professionals and teens.

http://tobaccofreekids.org/
This web site gets all the current anti-smoking information. Take a quiz, read special reports about tobacco, and plenty more.

http://scienceu.fsu.edu/
Find out how a smoking addiction affects your body, read helpful advice to help stop smoking, and much, much more.

http://www.sk.lung.ca/education/
student/student.html
This website helps you learn about your lungs and how tobacco harms them.

www.thetruth.com
This site designed for young people lets them learn about the 2001 Truth Tour, read up-to-date information about tobacco and tobacco companies, and ways young people can get involved with the fight against tobacco and its manufacturers as well as helping friends and family not to smoke.

www.cdc.gov/tobacco/edumat.htm
National Center for Chronic Disease Prevention and Health Promotion
Provides data, tables, results of smoking surveys, and plenty of educational material.

Sources used for this book

Blair, C. *Predicting the Onset of Smoking in Boys and Girls*. Social Science and Medicine, 1989.

Wilkinson, J. *Tobacco: The Facts Behind the Smokescreen*. New York: Penguin, 1986.

Action on Smoking and Health (ASH), various articles and pamphlets.

National Center for Chronic Disease Prevention and Health Promotion, website British American Tobacco, website and promotional materials.

World Health Organization, *Smoke Free Europe*, 1989.

Smoking and Pollution, materials published by the Health Education Authority Family Smoking Project.

Articles in the *British Medical Journal, Health Education Journal, New Scientist*.

Glossary

addiction a condition in which a person takes a drug regularly and cannot stop taking it without experiencing symptoms of withdrawal.

alveoli (singular alveolus) tiny air-filled sacs in the lungs, with walls one–cell thick and surrounded by capillaries. They provide a large surface area over which oxygen and carbon dioxide can be exchanged between air and blood.

bronchitis an inflammation of the bronchi and bronchioles, leading to difficulty in breathing.

cancer a malignant growth or tumor produced by the uncontrolled division of cells.

carbon monoxide a colorless, odorless gas released when carbon-containing substances are burned, for example, tobacco and fossil fuels.

carcinogen a chemical that has been found to cause cancer.

cardiovascular relating to the heart and circulation.

chemotherapy the treating of cancerous growths or tumors using powerful drugs that seek out and kill cancerous cells.

dependence a condition in which the body relies on the presence of a substance.

dopamine a chemical released by nerve cells in the brain. It affects the brain processes that control movement, emotional responses, and the ability to experience pain and pleasure.

hormone a chemical messenger, produced by endocrine or ductless glands in the body, which affects other parts of the body. For example, the hormone adrenaline is produced by the adrenal gland and affects the heart.

menopause the time during which a woman's periods gradually stop. It is a time of great hormonal change and adjustment.

menstruation the monthly discharge of blood from the lining of the uterus in women. Each cycle lasts about 28 days.

nicotine a poisonous chemical found in tobacco, with addictive properties. It can be lethal if injected into the body, but it is not lethal when inhaled.

oncogene a gene that can change a normal cell into a cancerous one.

passive smoking the inhalation of cigarette smoke by a non-smoker, which can affect his or her health.

peer-group pressure the influence of an individual or individuals on the behavior of people of the same age or interests.

sidestream smoke smoke released from the lit end of a cigarette that is not inhaled by the smoker.

withdrawal the process of ceasing to take an addictive drug, which may be accompanied by unpleasant side effects.

Index